CELEBRATING HOLIDAYS

Groundhog Day

by Rachel Grack

BELLWETHER MEDIA • MINNEAPOLIS, MN

Note to Librarians, Teachers, and Parents:

Blastoff! Readers are carefully developed by literacy experts and combine standards-based content with developmentally appropriate text.

Level 1 provides the most support through repetition of high-frequency words, light text, predictable sentence patterns, and strong visual support.

Level 2 offers early readers a bit more challenge through varied simple sentences, increased text load, and less repetition of high-frequency words.

Level 3 advances early-fluent readers toward fluency through increased text and concept load, less reliance on visuals, longer sentences, and more literary language.

Level 4 builds reading stamina by providing more text per page, increased use of punctuation, greater variation in sentence patterns, and increasingly challenging vocabulary.

Level 5 encourages children to move from "learning to read" to "reading to learn" by providing even more text, varied writing styles, and less familiar topics.

Whichever book is right for your reader, Blastoff! Readers are the perfect books to build confidence and encourage a love of reading that will last a lifetime!

This edition first published in 2018 by Bellwether Media, Inc.

No part of this publication may be reproduced in whole or in part without written permission of the publisher. For information regarding permission, write to Bellwether Media, Inc., Attention: Permissions Department, 5357 Penn Avenue South, Minneapolis, MN 55419.

Library of Congress Cataloging-in-Publication Data

Names: Koestler-Grack, Rachel A., 1973-
Title: Groundhog Day / by Rachel Grack.
Description: Minneapolis, MN : Bellwether Media, Inc., 2018. | Series: Blastoff! readers. Celebrating holidays | Audience: Age 5-8. | Audience: K to grade 3. | Includes bibliographical references and index.
Identifiers: LCCN 2016052723 (print) | LCCN 2017015897 (ebook) | ISBN 9781626176201 (hardcover : alk. paper) | ISBN 9781681033501 (ebook)
Subjects: LCSH: Groundhog Day–Juvenile literature.
Classification: LCC GT4995.G76 (ebook) | LCC GT4995.G76 K64 2018 (print) | DDC 394.261–dc23
LC record available at https://lccn.loc.gov/2016052723

Editor: Christina Leighton   Designer: Lois Stanfield

Printed in the United States of America, North Mankato, MN.

Table of Contents

Groundhog Day Is Here!

People wake up to a cloudy morning. They are happy the sun is not shining.

GROUNDHOG DAY

As early as 1886, German immigrants here observed Groundhog Day and established the Punxsutawney Groundhog Club in 1899. According to folklore, if the hibernating groundhog-known as Punxsutawney Phil-leaves its burrow on February 2 and sees its shadow, there will be six more weeks of winter. The legend is based on a European custom predicting the length of winter by weather conditions on Candlemas, an ancient Christian festival.

Winter may be over soon.
It is Groundhog Day!

What Is Groundhog Day?

A groundhog **forecasts** the weather on Groundhog Day.

Six more weeks of winter will come if it sees its shadow. Spring is near if it does not.

Identify a Groundhog

Other name: woodchuck

rounded ears

large front teeth

brown — or gray fur

short, bushy tail

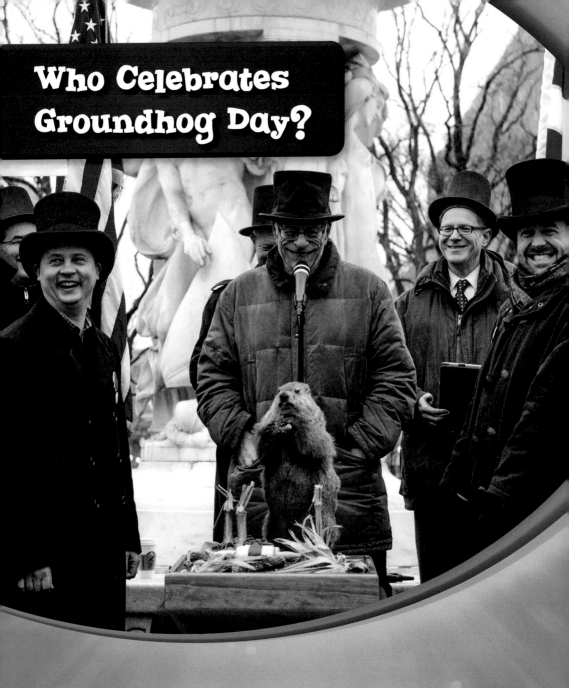

Who Celebrates Groundhog Day?

Groundhog Day is mostly celebrated in the United States.

Some states have their own **traditions**. Canada also enjoys Groundhog Day.

Groundhog Range Map

Canada

United States

groundhog range

Groundhog Day Beginnings

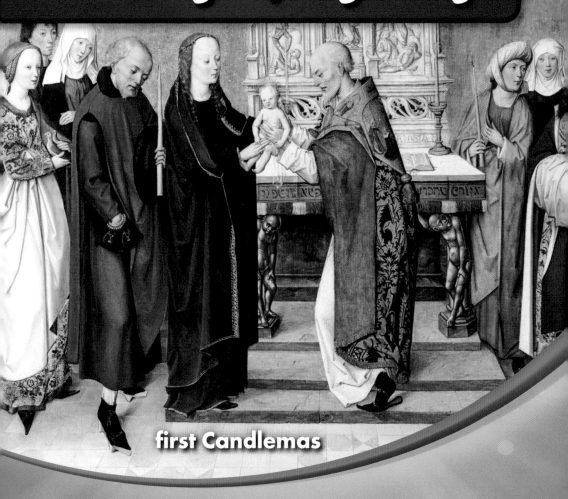

first Candlemas

Groundhog Day came from a **Christian** holiday called Candlemas. Sunshine on this holiday meant a longer winter.

People also used animals that **hibernate** to tell the weather on this day.

brown bear and cub

German **immigrants** brought the tradition to the United States. They decided to use a groundhog.

groundhog

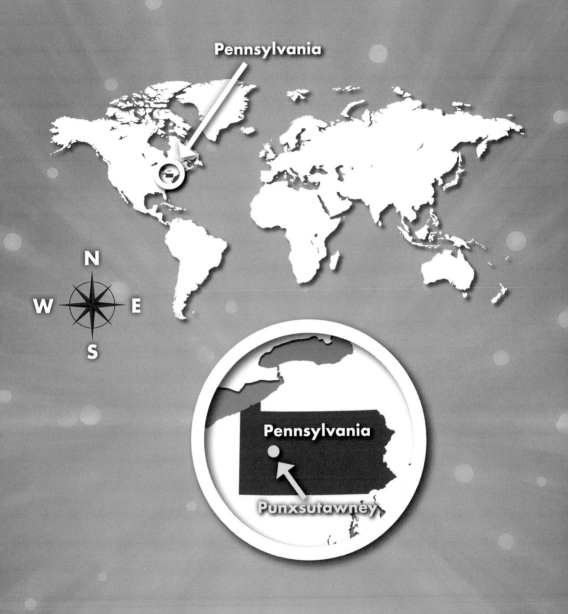

The first **official** Groundhog Day took place in Punxsutawney, Pennsylvania, in 1887.

Time to Celebrate

Groundhog Day takes place on February 2 every year.

Some places have celebrations that last more than a day. Pennsylvania holds a big event!

Groundhog Day Traditions!

People watch groundhogs to see if they **cast** shadows. Some states keep pet groundhogs. The most famous groundhog is Phil from Pennsylvania.

Punxsutawney
Phil™

Make a Pop-Up Groundhog Puppet

Take this puppet outside on Groundhog Day to see if it makes a shadow!

What You Need:
- brown or white paper
- pencil
- markers or crayons
- scissors
- popsicle or craft stick
- glue
- paper cup

What You Do:

1. Draw a rectangle on the construction paper, 2 inches by 4 inches. Draw a groundhog inside the rectangle. Color it as desired.
2. Cut out the groundhog.
3. Glue it to one end of the craft sti⟨ck⟩ The other end is the puppet han⟨dle⟩
4. Cut a slit in the bottom of the paper cup.
5. Push the handle through the slit.
6. Make the groundhog pop up fro⟨m⟩ its burrow!

1

3

5

Many people visit Gobbler's Knob in Pennsylvania.

There, Phil tells the Groundhog Club president the forecast. Phil speaks in the "Groundhogese" language.

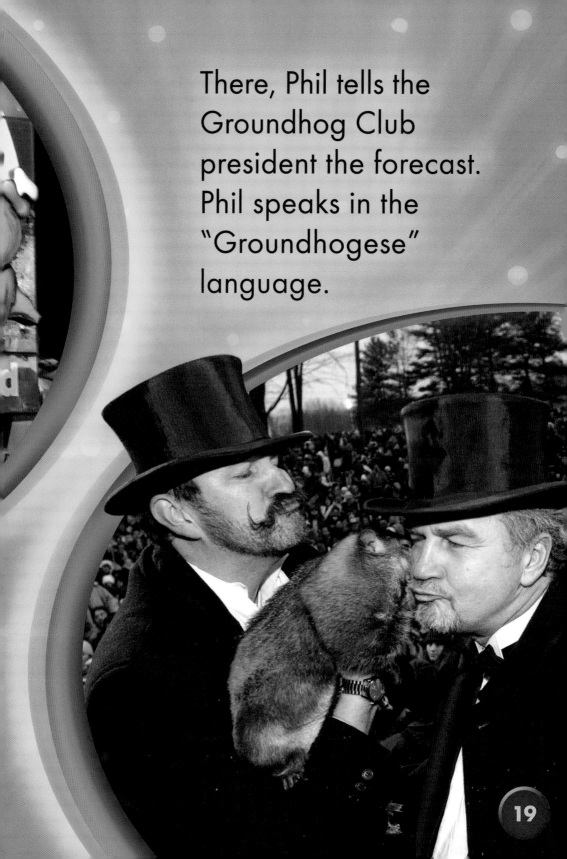

Families visit celebrations in town. They eat snacks and shop.

Some people dance at the
Groundhog Ball. Cloudy
or sunny, people enjoy
Groundhog Day!

Glossary

cast—to make and send out

Christian—related to Christianity; Christians are people who believe in the teachings of Jesus Christ and the Christian Bible.

forecasts—says what may happen in the future

hibernate—to spend the winter sleeping or resting

immigrants—people who come from one country to live in another

official—publicly known

traditions—customs, ideas, and beliefs handed down from one generation to the next

To Learn More

AT THE LIBRARY

Cella, Clara. *Groundhog Day.* Mankato, Minn.: Capstone Press, 2013.

Herrington, Lisa M. *Groundhog Day.* New York, N.Y.: Children's Press, 2014.

Smith, Maximilian. *What Is Groundhog Day?* New York, N.Y.: Gareth Stevens Publishing, 2016.

ON THE WEB

Learning more about Groundhog Day is as easy as 1, 2, 3.

1. Go to www.factsurfer.com.

2. Enter "Groundhog Day" into the search box.

3. Click the "Surf" button and you will see a list of related web sites.

With factsurfer.com, finding more information is just a click away.

Index

The images in this book are reproduced through the courtesy of: impr2003, front cover; fdastudillo, pp. 4, 18-19; Brian E Kushner, pp. 4-5; All Canada Photos/ Alamy, pp. 6-7; WILDLIFE GmbH/ Alamy, p. 7; Xinhua/ Alamy, pp. 8-9; Art Collection 2/ Alamy, pp. 10-11; Arterra Picture Library/ Alamy, p. 11; Holly Kuchera, p. 12; DAVID MAXWELL/ EPA/ Newscom, pp. 14-15, 20; The Punxsutawney Groundhog Club, p. 15; REUTERS/ Alamy, pp. 16, 19; Lois Stanfield, p. 17 (all photos); Krymouski, p. 17 (illustration); GEOFF ROBINS/ REUTERS/ Newscom, pp. 20-21; Michael Burrell, p. 22.